One day, a student went to
see the great teacher Chao-chou
and asked, "Does a dog (like me)
have Buddha nature or not?"

And Chao-chou said, "Mu."

Wisdom Publications
199 Elm Street
Somerville, MA 02144 USA
wisdompubs.org

Library of Congress Cataloging-in-Publication Data
Names: Cordova, James V., 1966– author. | Morse, Mark, illustrator.
Title: The story of Mu / James Cordova ; Illustrated by Mark Morse.
Description: Somerville, MA : Wisdom Publications, 2016.
Identifiers: LCCN 2015026553| ISBN 1614292205 (pbk. : alk. paper) | ISBN
   9781614292388 (Ebook)
Subjects: LCSH: Zen stories. | Koan.
Classification: LCC BQ9264 .C67 2016 | DDC 294.3/4432—dc23
LC record available at http://lccn.loc.gov/2015026553

ISBN 978-1-61429-220-3   ebook ISBN 978-1-61429-238-8

20 19 18 17 16
5 4 3 2 1

Artwork by Mark T. Morse. Cover design by Philip Pascuzzo. Interior design by Philip Pascuzzo. Set in Klinic Slab 18/25.2.

The Story of Mu

JAMES CORDOVA

Illustrated by MARK MORSE

Wisdom

For my mom, Theresa Cordova,
who always blessed me with her love.
—J. C.

For my father, who taught me how to draw,
my friend George, who kept me drawing,
and my family, who gave me the space
and time to accomplish this work.
—M. M.

I want to play with a story, a fable, or a myth—whatever we call a story when we know it is just a story and can treat it lightly, like a game.

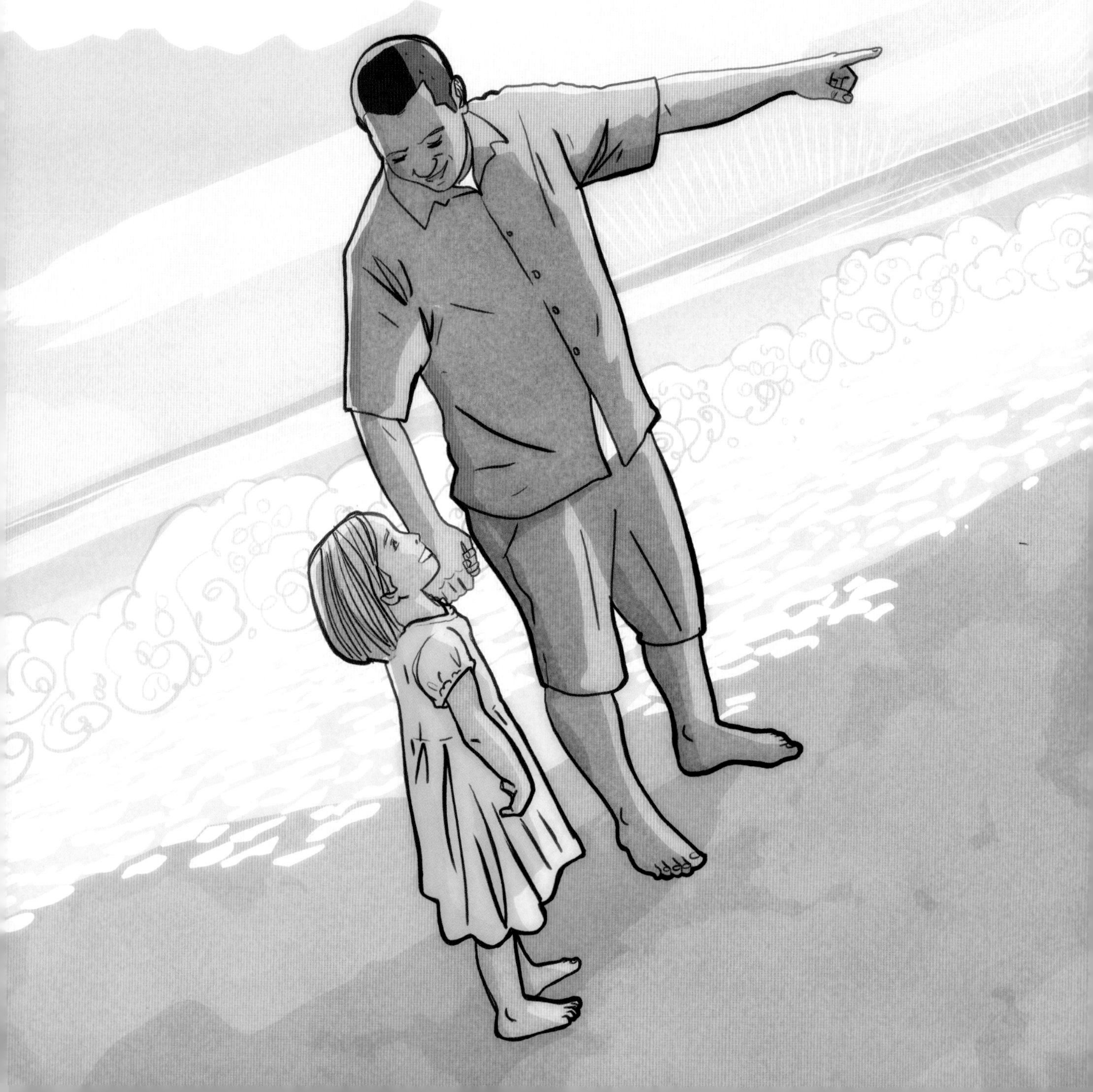

We could look at the serious nature of the story
or we can just choose to enjoy it
and leave its deeper significance alone.

In the beginning,
in the beginning before the beginning,
there was Mu.

And Mu was Mu and that was that
and it was good.

Before time,
Mu was Mu
and that was that
and all was well.

One day Mu noticed that if she turned just so,
she could be space and time and matter.
That was fun. She kept at it for a long while.

Mu was Mu
and time and space and matter
and it was wonderful.

Later, she noticed that if she bent herself around *this* way, she could be stars and planets and gravity and light and vast distances.

That was fun too, so she kept at it for a while.
Mu was Mu and stars and planets and gravity and
vast distances, and it was profound and it whirled.

For eons Mu frolicked,
delighting in her capacity to bend and twist
and scamper into this form and that form—

light and dark, here and there,
hot, cold, near, far, big, small,
together and complicated, apart and simple.

One day she was mucking around as the "vast primordial stew" and backflipped herself into life. Now *this* was fun. Something new and wonderful to be.

She played at folding herself into life in billions of ways.
And Mu was Mu and time and matter and life,
and it roared and danced and sang.

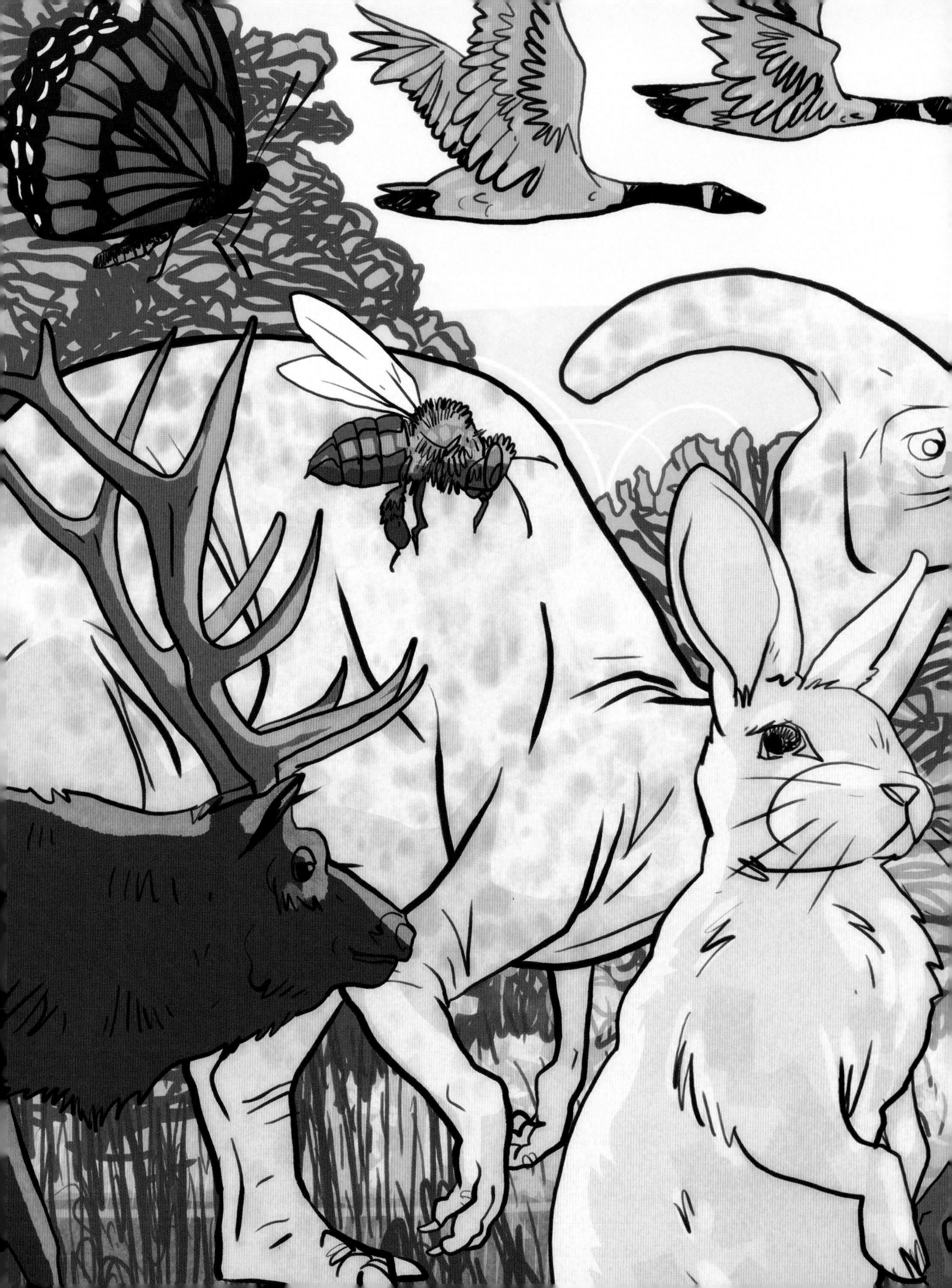

After a great deal of diving and dancing,
she sashayed herself into a human being.

Quite a thing. Quite a thing.

As a human being
she found she could be
thought, emotion, sensation,
perception, mental reaction,
consciousness, and attention.

Mu was delighted.

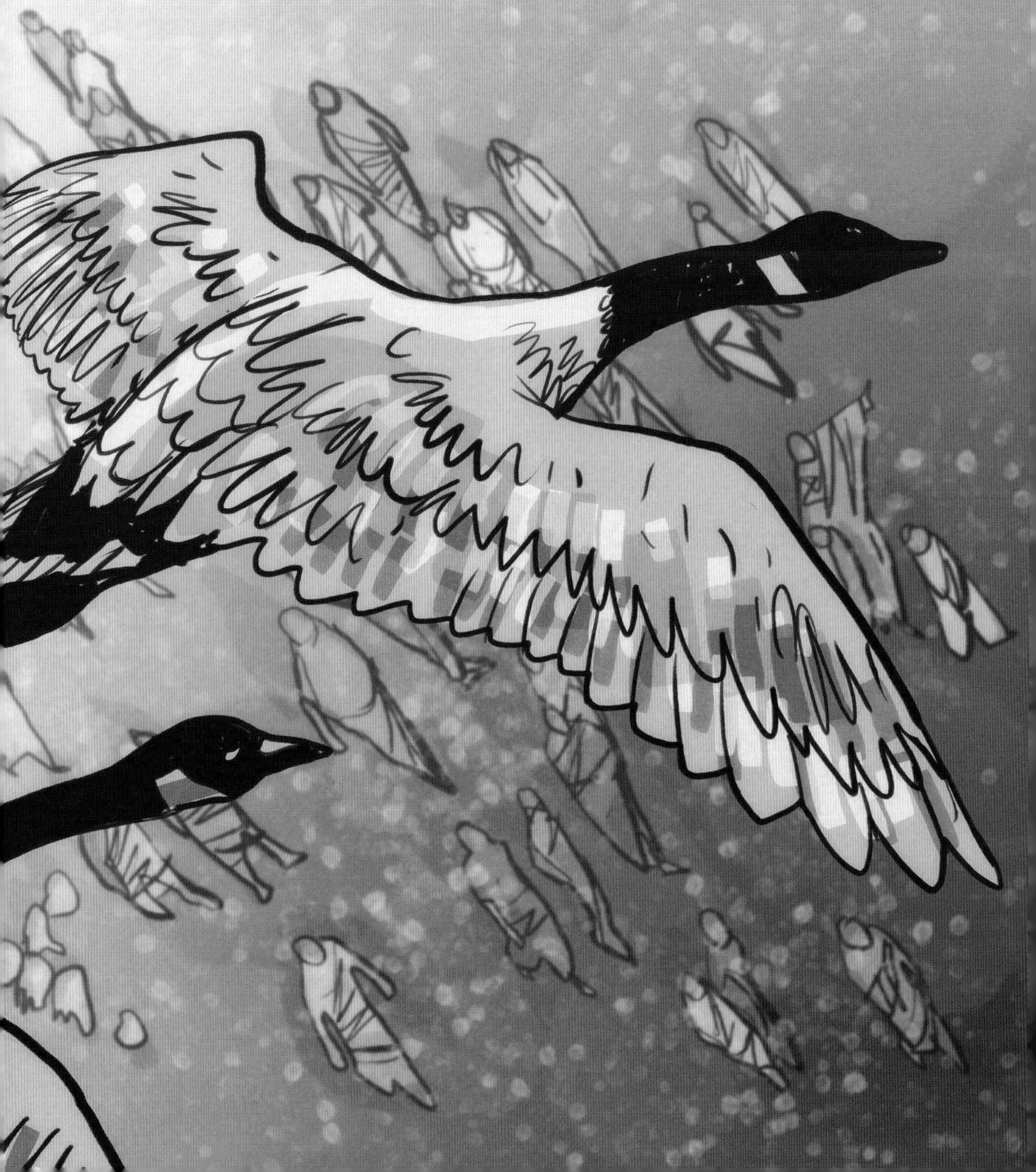

And then a funny thing happened.
Mu folded herself into a labyrinth in the mind.

And in the labyrinth she discovered if she reached behind her in just this certain way she could become the delusion of separation, of two-ness, and in that particular mind she became lost and forgot her Mu-ness.

Now Mu found she
folded herself into lonely
and separate and sad, into misery
and suffering of all kinds.

All the minds got lost.

Separation spread like a plague.
Mu forgot that she was Mu.
Everything became
unconnected and afraid.

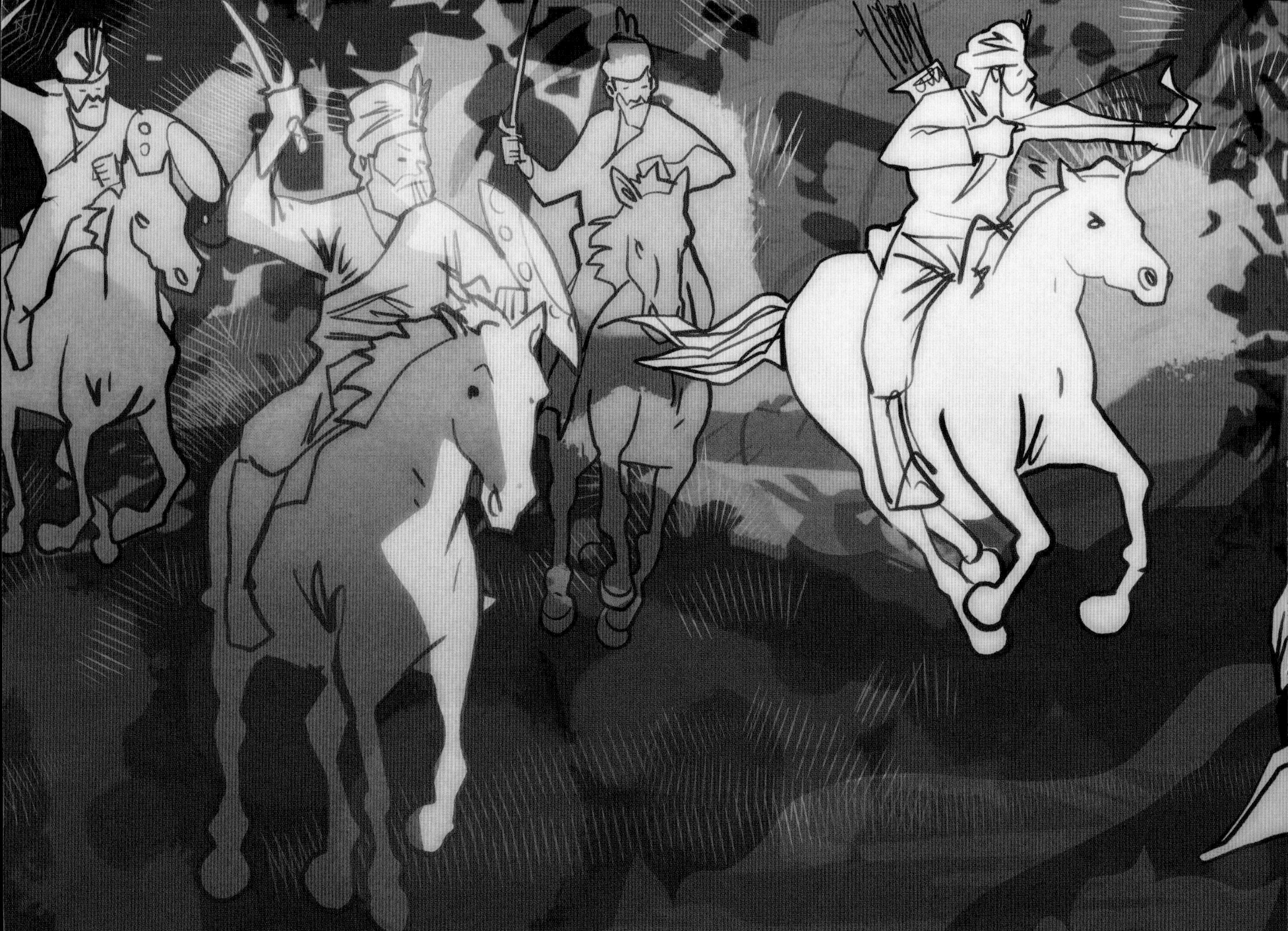

Human beings were trapped inside this labyrinth of delusion. Without their Mu-ness, they turned against each other.

"I am me and you are other."
"These things are mine and those things are yours."

Greed and anger were born out of delusion. Then came the idea of good and evil, killing, stealing, disrespect, and indignity, speaking falsely, finding fault, praising self, and abusing others.

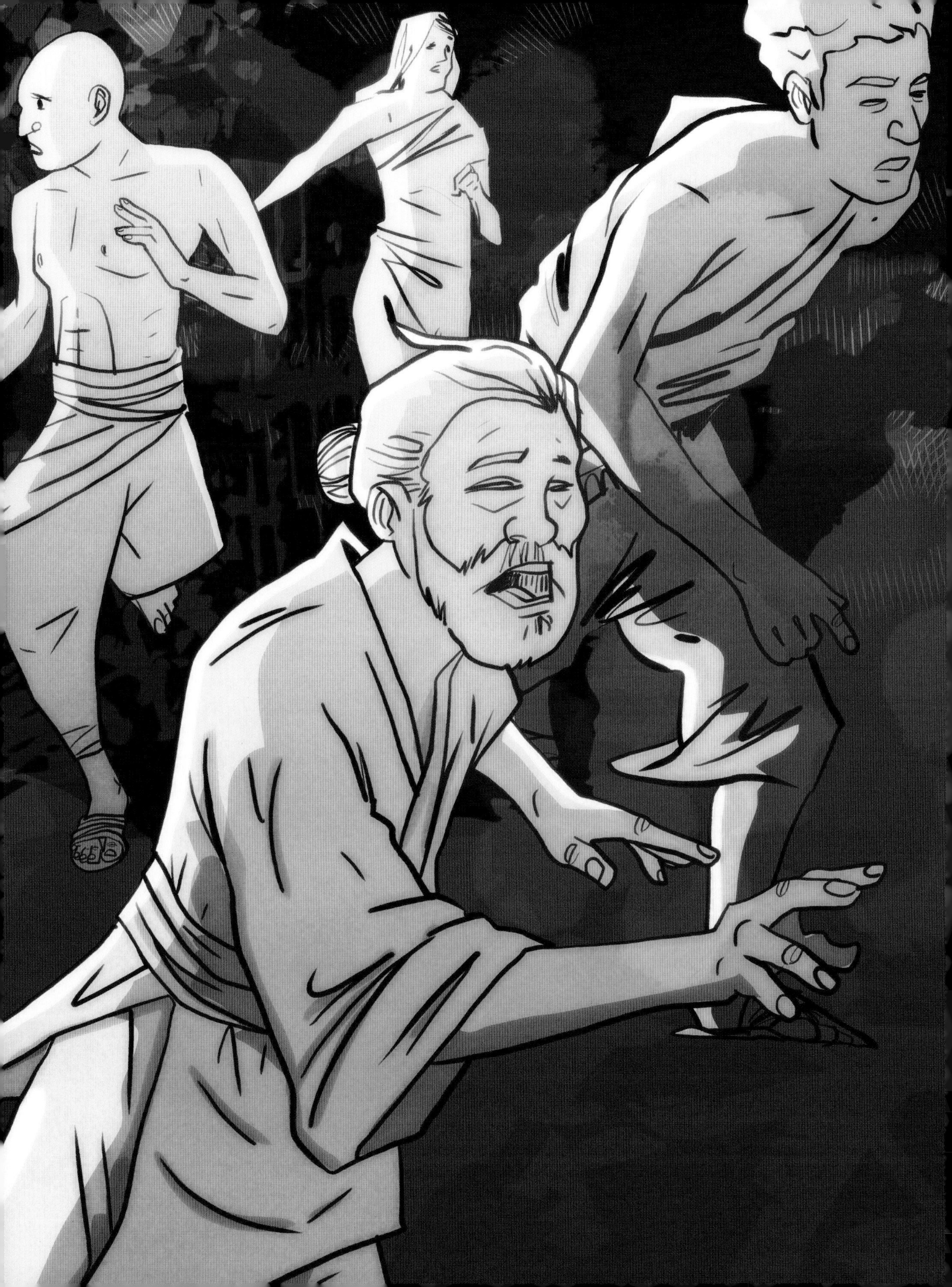

It was this way
for many, many years.

One day, deep in the mist of separation,
a baby boy was born in the woods of Kapilavastu.

And at the moment of birth, for just a heartbeat, before the labyrinth settled in, he remembered he was Mu.

So desperate was Mu to escape the labyrinth and wake up,
she yanked her newborn body up and waddled forward,
pointing up to the sky and down to the earth and crying,
"I am only One."

People thought it was surprising and cute,
but no one understood.

Many years later, sitting quietly under a tree,
determined to follow this vague, dreamlike, barely
remembered whiff of the truth, that boy, now a man,
quite by accident dropped out of his own way
and Mu woke up and knew herself again.

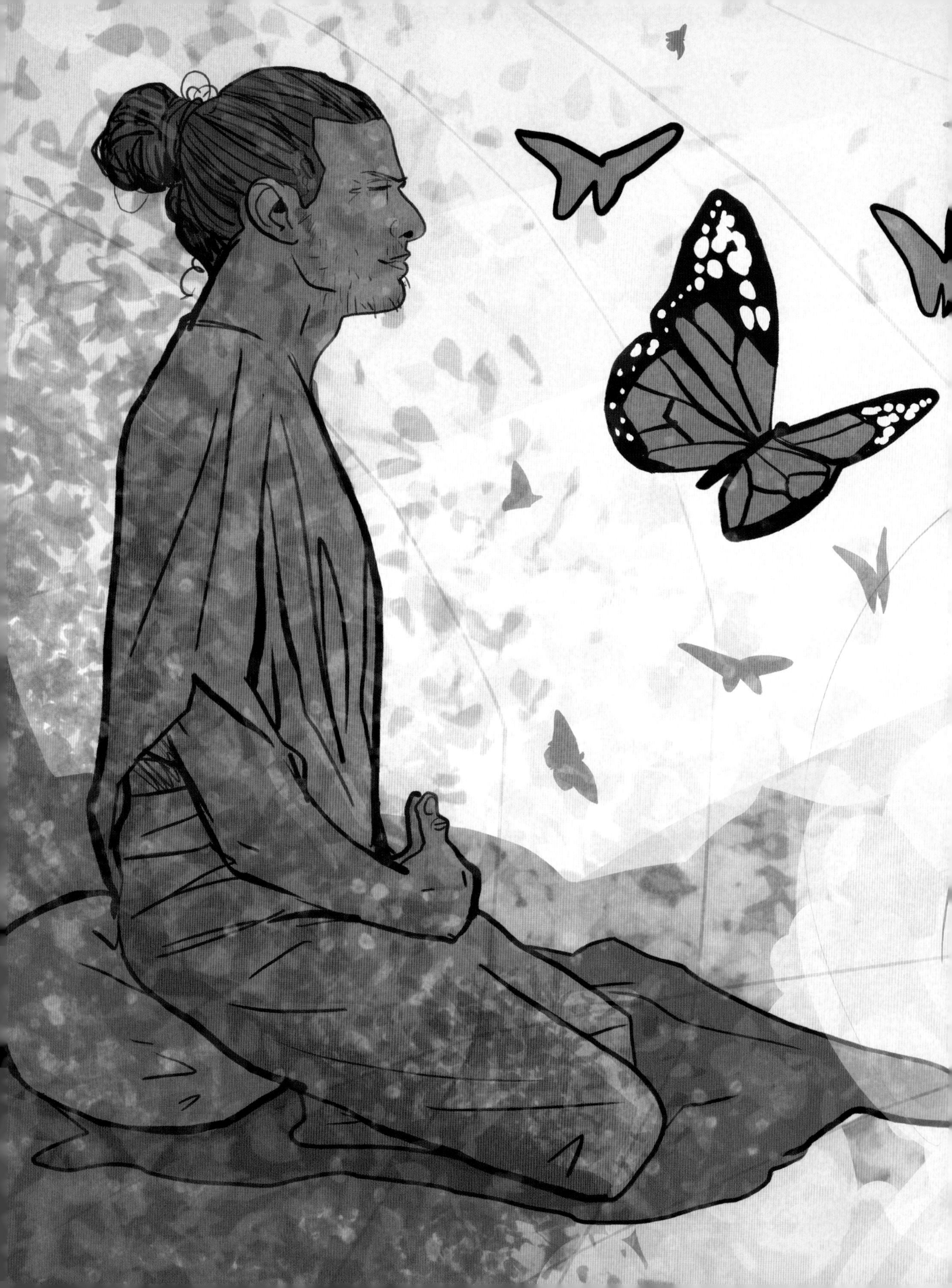

I am Mu! Mu is Mu! Mu is time and matter and vast space
and all beings everywhere! And the earth shook
and the trees sang and Mu was so delighted that she wept.

And when she was done, she thought,
"They must all be freed."

And she set off to help them see.

Waking up flowed out of this Buddha,
the One Who Woke Up, like a thin stream,

and the stream became a wide creek,
and the creek became a mighty river.

And that river has flowed ever since—
sometimes wide and strong, sometimes thin but clear.
And everywhere it goes people wake up
and know that they are Mu—

that they are Mu
and time and space
and vast distances
and joy and life and love
and this-ness and thus-ness,

without flaw and perfect from the very beginning,
before the beginning.

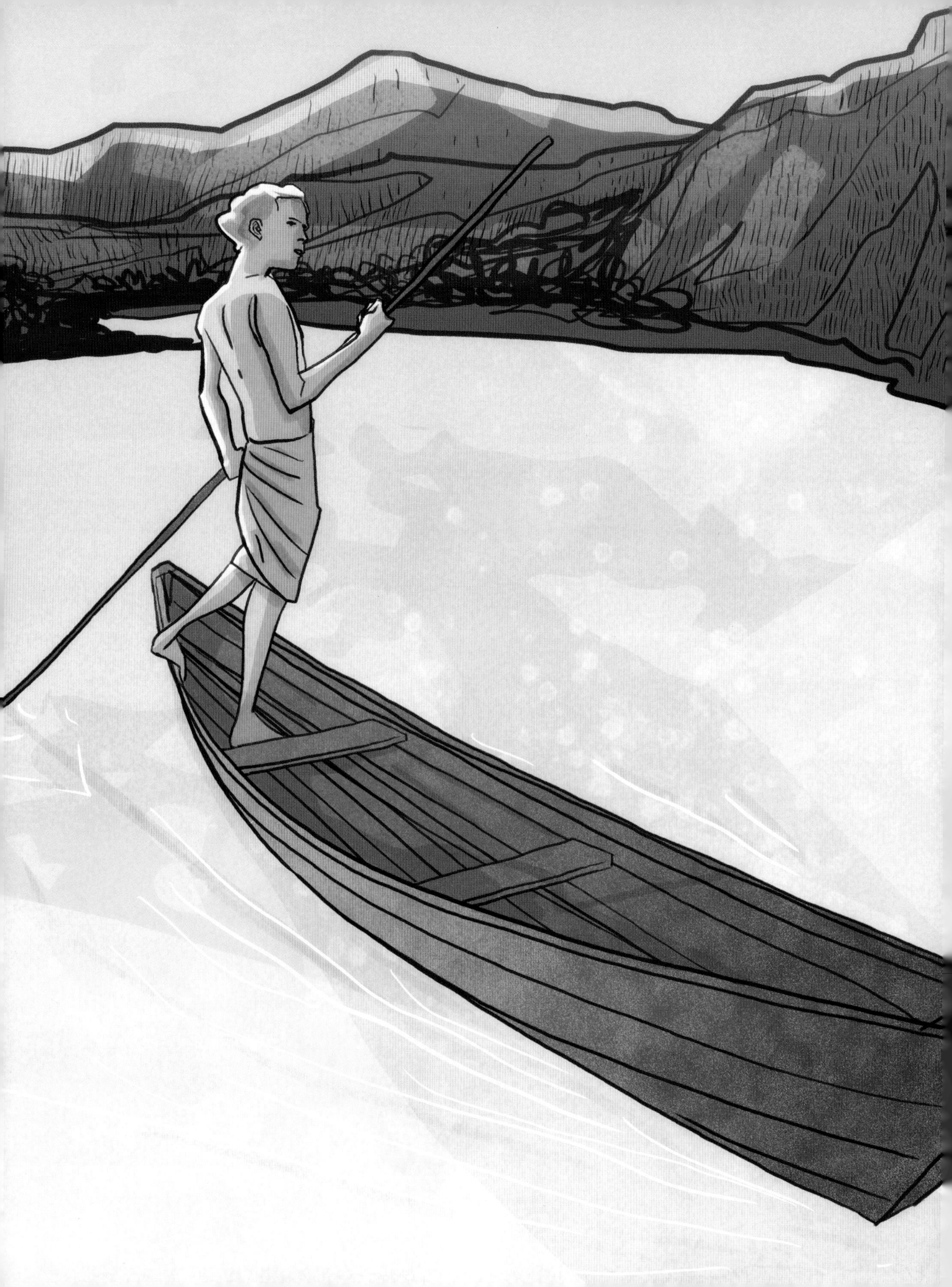

And now this river flows to you.

Mu has lovingly shaped herself into this book
and your hands and these eyes and this mind.

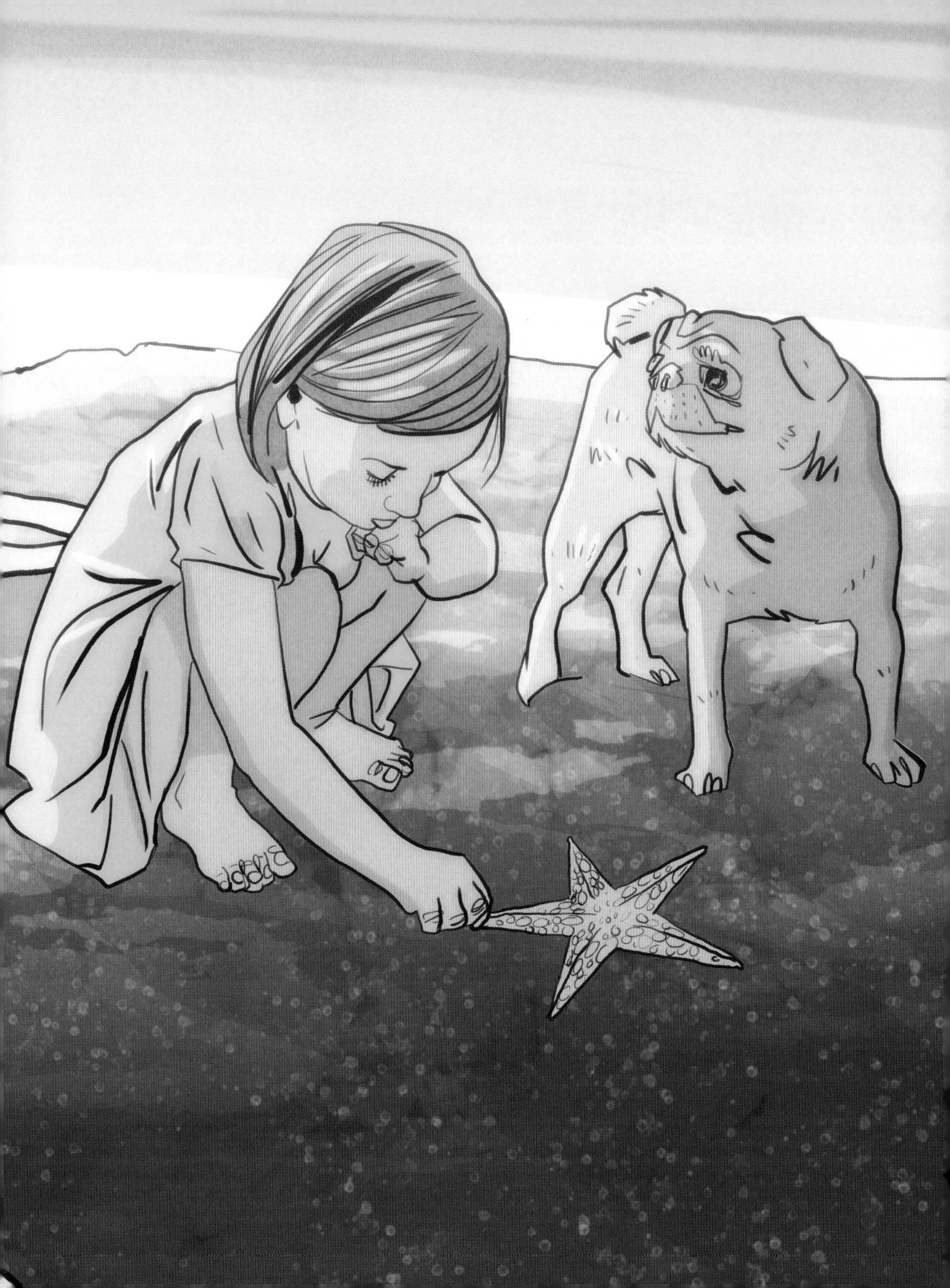

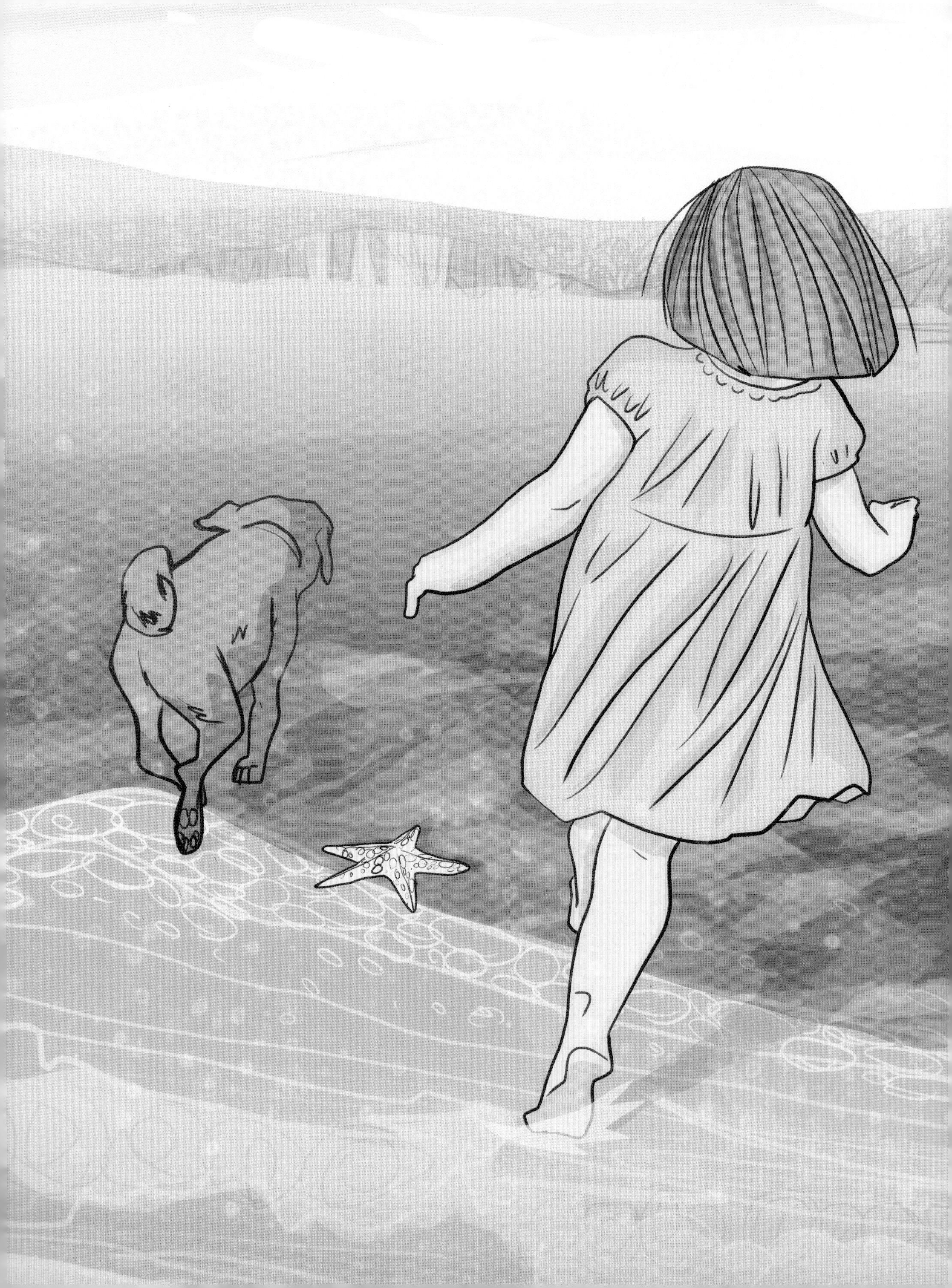

Wake up little Mu.

Wake up…

One day, a student went to see the
great teacher Chao-chou
and asked, "Does a dog (like me)
have Buddha nature or not?"

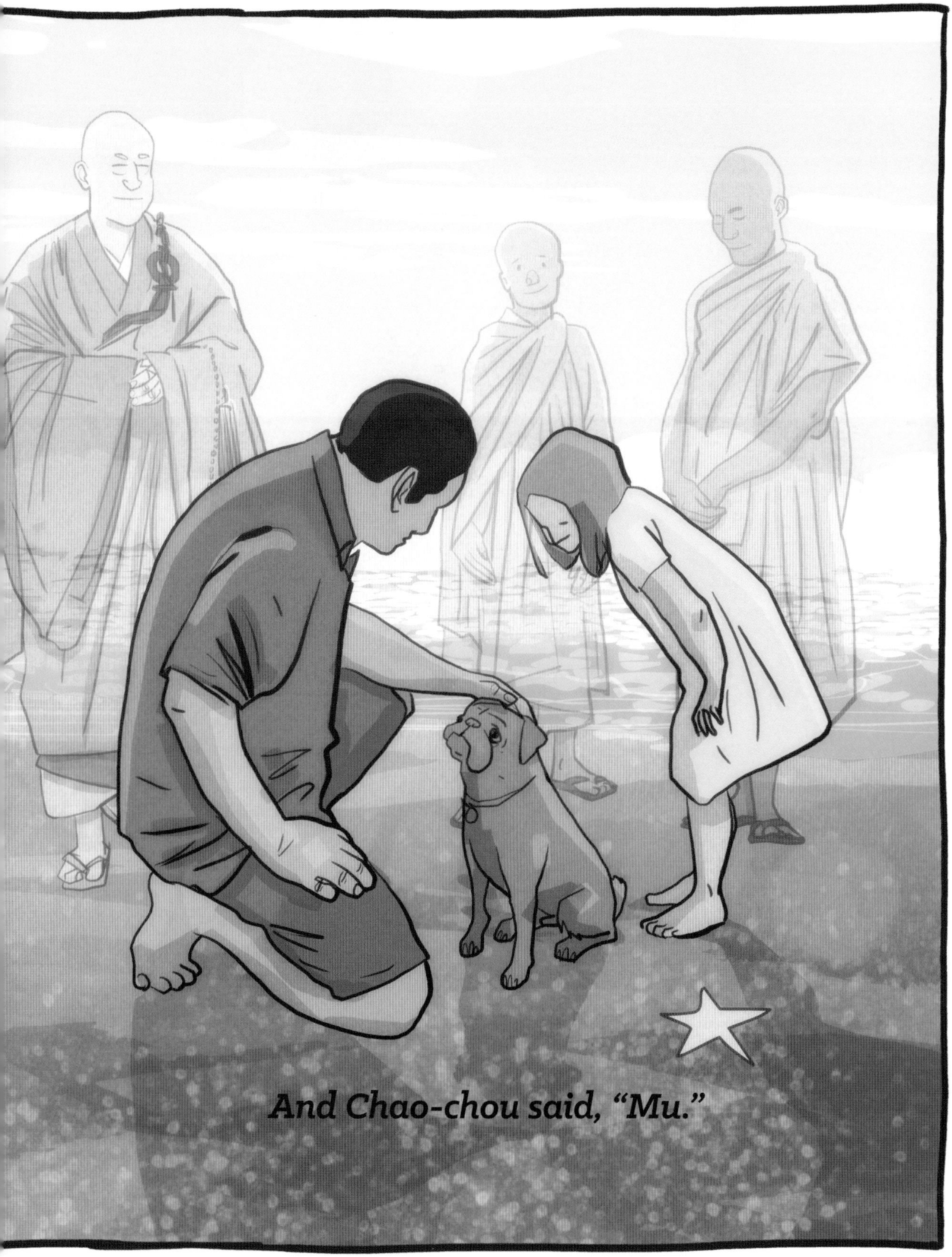
And Chao-chou said, "Mu."

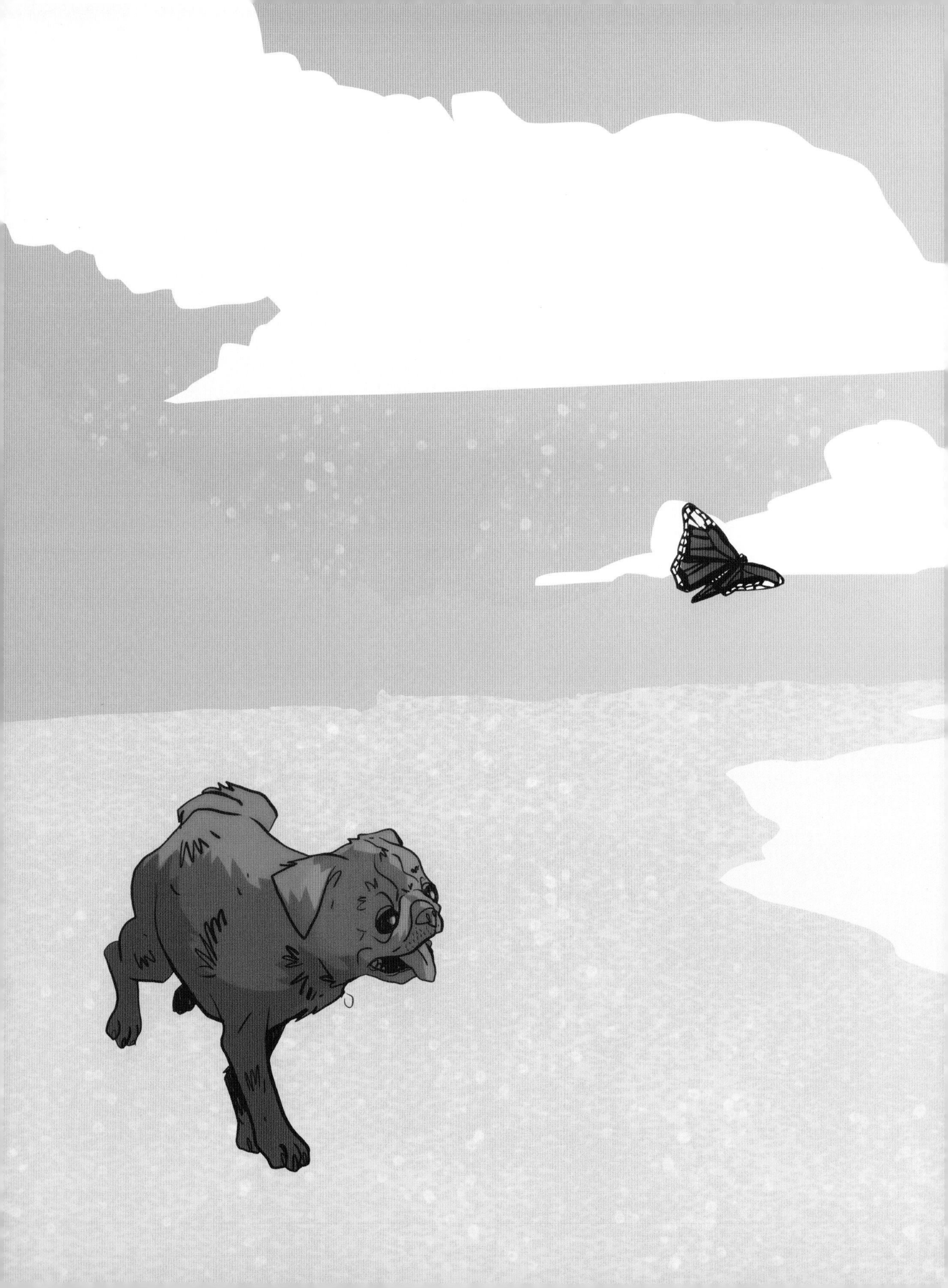

On the Utter, Complete, Total Ordinariness of Mu

James Ishmael Ford

What we're promised by the teachers of the Zen Way is that we and all things, we, you and I, and every blessed thing, share the same root.

Mu is just a noise. It is a placeholder. But what it holds for us is a way of being in the world, that in fact we're always experiencing. It's always here. We just don't notice it.

The catch is that the other way of being in the world, of slicing and dicing, of separating and weighing and judging, well, it's important too, it's useful. In fact seeing into our shared place isn't particularly useful. It doesn't pay the bills. It doesn't get us a partner. It's in fact the most countercultural thing we can be about. And so, even though we are surrounded by it, often, usually, its very existence slips into the back of our human consciousness. And even though it is the background of our lives, we come to forget it.

But rarely do we forget it completely; it is our common heritage, our birthright as we enter into this universe. It peeks out at us in our dreams. It whispers to us in the dark. It beckons in the playing of children and the touch of a kiss. And it appears even in some very rough patches of our lives, sometimes the roughest. You never know when you'll notice it.

Now I want to be clear here. Each of these phrases I've just used are metaphors, pointers. Don't look for a thing here. Just open your heart and mind.

Also—and this is important—there is a pernicious oneness, experienced in many ways, although most often as a projection of our egos. Here we come to think our sense of self, our ego, is the great One itself. And while there is a truth in that observation, the lie of it becomes

obvious in the violence, subtle or otherwise, that arises out of our mounting defenses of this false one against the assaults of the world, all those endlessly arising other aspects of the One that are denied.

That said, back to the matter of Mu and its utter uselessness. If you've presented yourself to a Zen hall, if you've come for an interview with a Zen teacher, you're probably looking for an answer to some question about your life. There's been some nagging thing at the bottom of your heart, the back of your head. Something, perhaps only the smallest thing, hints that the life lived up to this point isn't enough. Or even that phrase "not enough" doesn't quite express it; those of us who come to Zen often find some sense of dis-ease haunts us.

So perhaps you're ready to let the call of gain, of success one way or another, fall down a notch or two. Perhaps you're ready for something that has no value. And so you take up our disciplines of sitting down, shutting up, and paying attention. Sitting is a good thing. Lots of sitting sometimes is a very good thing. (Though sometimes lots of sitting isn't.) And taking up the hard way is sometimes very necessary. Throwing our hearts and bodies into the practice, sometimes, can be the most important thing we can choose to do. There is a place for the style of intense practice likened to a red-hot iron ball.

But, actually, here's the secret: All you need do is step out of your own way. That's the only problem. We stand in our own way. It's already here. It's always here. Perhaps you first noticed it as a child, maybe as an adolescent. It's taught in Buddhism, and Taoism, and Judaism, and Islam, and Christianity. It's found somewhere in all religions. And it's found in the hearts of people who claim no religion. It is as close as the throbbing in your jugular vein. It is proclaimed in the next breath you draw. It's found canoeing in Maine and it's found changing a diaper.

The pointers are everywhere. In that most Zen-like of Western spiritual testaments, the Gospel of Thomas, the sage Jesus declares that if you want to see him, cut a board in two, or pick up a stone. Saying you can find it when you cleave a board or pick up a stone doesn't mean there's some magical board out there waiting to be found or one rock is more precious than all others. Rather it is just this piece of wood.

It is just this pebble.
It is just this breath.
It is just this Mu.
Breathing.
Mu.
Presenting.
Mu.
Nowhere else.
Mu.
Easy as falling off a log.

* * * *

Sitting with Mu is best done in companionship with a koan teacher, who can act as a loving guide, someone who is both a sounding board and who directs you back, over and over again, to what is true, right here and now.

I hope that you have found inspiration for your own Zen practice.

At this point, it's up to you.

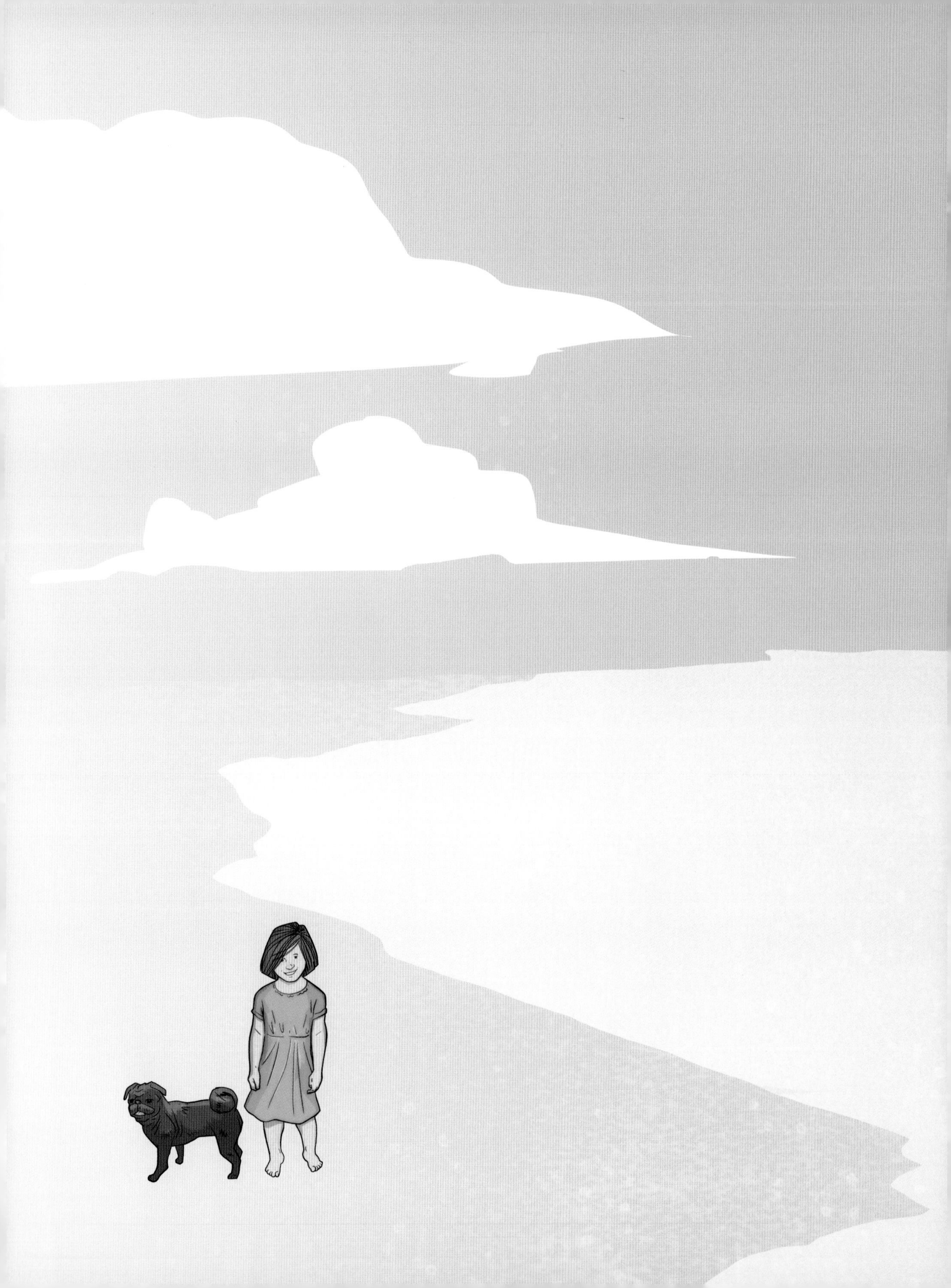

The Art of Mu
Mark Morse

The text for James Cordova's *The Story of Mu* suggests to the imagination of an illustrator a vast kaleidoscope of potential imagery. The story itself, which touches upon the evolution of time, space, matter, species, and consciousness, offers the opportunity to convey seemingly the entire breadth of existence. But it also frames that evolution within the warm, personal context of a parent telling a child a story. Then again, the story being told is no ordinary story, but a story based on a Zen koan that's been perplexing students of Zen for the past twelve centuries! From an artistic perspective, *The Story of Mu* offers "the whole kit and caboodle," as they say.

Visually, I was drawn to the sense of animation, migration, and transformation depicted in the story. It was my intention to represent this sense of movement through reoccurring themes: water running from mountains to oceans, the movement of butterflies and geese, and the use of a slowly evolving color palette to convey major thematic transitions. I also enjoyed the concept of a fantastical story that was not fantasy. The idea of the "fantastic, yet everyday" prompted me to look for mythical imagery within our known world.

The Story of Mu was a joy to play with visually. It could have been illustrated, conveyed, and relayed in so many different ways. As the artist, all of creation was literally available to me as my reference material. I could have used images from any time or place, since the beginning without beginning. The greatest challenge I faced was limiting my creativity to the space available within the pages of this book.

As a father and Zen practitioner, I am deeply aware of how challenging it is to communicate what one comes to know of the world to others, let alone one's children. Having the opportunity to depict that message through illustration was a significant and special experience for me.

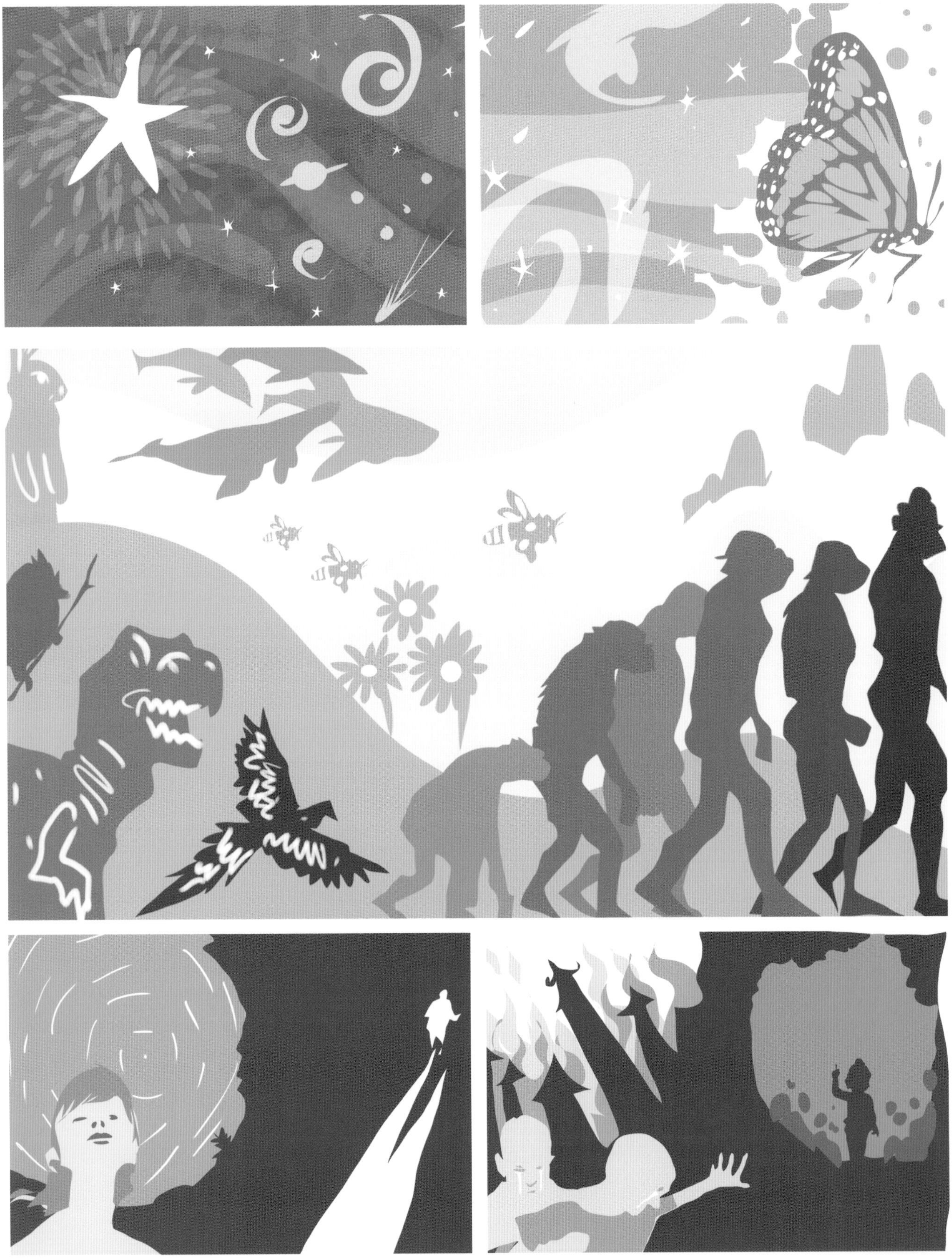

PREVIOUS PAGE, FACING PAGE, AND THIS PAGE: *The Story of Mu* provided a vexing challenge to would-be illustrators: How do you create a captivating visual narrative about a character that cannot be depicted? In his simple, nine-page black and white proposal that begins and ends with a parent and child at the edge of the sea, Mark Morse deftly captured both the cosmic scope and the personal message that the story conveys, and breathed life into Mu.

Many years later, sitting quietly under a tree, determined to follow this vague, dreamlike, barely remembered whiff of the Truth, that boy, now a man, quite by accident dropped out of his own way and Mu woke up and knew herself again.

THIS PAGE, FACING PAGE, AND FOLLOWING SPREAD:
As he developed his artwork for the story, Mark experimented
with an austere, graphic style and a colorful, almost Disney-esque
style, before settling on a happy medium between the two.

Mu folded herself into a Labyrinth in the Mind. And in the Labyrinth she discovered if she reached behind her in just this certain way she could come the Delusion of Separation, of Two-ness, and in that particular Mind she became Lost and forgot her Mu-ness.

Now mu found she folded herself into lonely, and separate, and sadness, misery and suffering of all kinds, all the minds got lost.

WAKING UP FLOWED OUT OF THIS BUDDHA,
THE ONE WHO WOKE UP, LIKE A THIN STREAM,
AND THE STREAM BECAME A WIDE CREEK,
AND THE CREEK BECAME A MIGHTY RIVER.

In early drafts, the lovable pug only appeared as a sketch on the culminating page of the book, along with the text of the Mu koan. As Mark's narrative style evolved over the course of working on the book, the dog was integrated more fully into the beach scenes that frame the story.

One day, a student went to see the great teacher Chao-chou and asked, 'Does a dog (like me) have Buddha nature or not? And Chao-chou said, 'Mu.'

Acknowledgments

I would never have written this book if it weren't for the many good people who supported me. I would like to thank my children, Ariana and Sam, who are my heart, and my partner Cindy, who created these two beautiful people with me, for their boundless love and support. I would also like to thank my teacher, Melissa Blacker Roshi—when the student is ready, the teacher appears. And I must also thank my other teachers, David Rynick Roshi, James Ford Roshi, and Josh Bartok, Sensei, because they are not-two.

James Cordova

About the Author

James Cordova

James Myosan Cordova received Dharma Entrustment, the beginning of formal Dharma transmission, from Melissa Myozen Blacker Roshi in December of 2013. He teaches with Blacker Roshi and David Rynick Roshi at the Boundless Way Temple in Worcester, Massachusetts, and is the guiding teacher for the Benevolent Street Zen Sangha in Providence, Rhode Island. James is also a professor and chair of the Department of Psychology at Clark University in Worcester, Massachusetts, and author of *The Marriage Checkup*.

About the Illustrator

Mark Morse

Illustrator Mark T. Morse lives in the Pacific Northwest with his wife, three daughters, and pug (who may bear some resemblance to the canine companion depicted in the book). His art-making life stretches back as far as he can remember, with his first art lessons coming from his artist father. Professionally, Mark works as a storyboard and conceptual illustrator at a digital consulting agency. Reflection on the stories and conundrums of Zen often occupy his personal creative efforts.

About the Essayist

James Ishmael Ford

James Ishmael Ford is the founding abbot of Boundless Way Zen. He is author of *If You're Lucky, Your Heart Will Break* and the coeditor (along with Melissa Myozen Blacker) of *The Book of Mu: Essential Writings on Zen's Most Famous Koan*. He lives in Long Beach, California.

Also Available from Wisdom Publications

The Book of Mu
Essential Writings on Zen's Most Important Koan
James Ishmael Ford
Melissa Myozen Blacker
Foreword by John Tarrant

"The most important of all koans finally gets the attention it deserves. For those considering koan study, or just curious about this unique spiritual practice, this is a very valuable book."—David R. Loy, author of *Money, Sex, War, Karma*

The Banyan Deer
A Parable of Courage and Compassion
Rafe Martin
Illustrated by Richard Wehrman

"*The Banyan Deer* shows that the lives of all living beings are equally important."
—Ogyen Trinley Dorje, the Seventeenth Karmapa

Sid
Anita Feng

"Feng tells us a story in luminous prose-poem paragraphs about an ordinary contemporary high school math teacher whose journey parallels the Buddha's. *Sid* reminds me that I, too, ordinary as I am, have Buddha nature, and that my seeking is not in vain."
—Susan Moon, coeditor of *The Hidden Lamp*

The World Is Made of Stories
David R. Loy

"Loy's book is like the self: layer after layer peels away, and the center is empty. But the pleasure is exactly in the exploration. At once Loy's most accessible and most philosophical work."—Alan Senauke for *Buddhadharma*

Wisdom Publications

Wisdom Publications is the leading publisher of classic and contemporary Buddhist books and practical works on mindfulness. To learn more about us or to explore our other books, please visit our website at wisdompubs.org or contact us as the address below.

Wisdom Publications
199 Elm Street
Somerville, MA 02144 USA

We are a 501(c)(3) organization, and donations in support of our mission are tax deductible.

Wisdom Publications is affiliated with the Foundation for the Preservation of the Mahayana Tradition (FPMT).